God's Guidance

&

How *to* Get It

(*The Seven Steps*)

To Include:

How God Guides

How *to be* Inexpressibly Happy

R. A. Torrey

God's Guidance
and How *to* Get It

–The Seven Steps –

"I will instruct thee and teach thee in the way which thou shalt go; I will guide thee with mine eye."[1]

"But if any of you lacketh wisdom, let him ask God, who giveth to all men liberally, and upbraideth not; and it shall be given him. But let him ask in faith, nothing doubting; for he that doubteth is like the surge of the sea driven by the wind and tossed. For let not that man think that he shall receive anything of the Lord; a double-minded man, unstable in all his ways."[2]

I. The Possibility and Blessedness of Being Guided by God

One of the greatest and most precious privileges of the believer is to have the guidance of God at every turn of life. One of the most important of all practical questions is how to get this guidance. There are many who say very positively that they are guided of God who are not so guided. The event proves that they are not so guided. Some months ago, a young woman informed me that she was guided of God to leave for Africa at a certain date and that God had given her positive assurance that the money would be provided for her to leave at that date. I was not at all sure that she was guided as she said that she was, and the event proved she was not; for the money was not furnished for her to leave at that date. As we see so many people apparently absolutely sure that God is guiding them when in the event it becomes clear that He is not, does it not prove that the supposed guidance of God is a fancy and not a fact? It does not. The fact that some people are confident that they are guided when they are not is no more evidence that there is no such thing as guidance than the fact that some

---

[1] *Ps. 32:8. -*
[2] *Jas 1:5-8 -*

people are sure they are saved when they are not is an evidence that there is no such thing as salvation, or assurance of salvation. The fact that some people are misled in no way proves that all people are misled. There is such a thing as guidance, and there is a way to get guidance. There is a way to avoid the illusions regarding guidance into which many fall through ignorance of the Word of God.

II. How to Get Guidance

We come now face to face with the question of how to get God's guidance. There are **Seven Steps**, clearly set forth in the Word of God, in the path that leads to God's guidance.

1. The first step toward obtaining God's guidance is that we accept the Lord Jesus Christ as our own personal Savior, and surrender to Him as our Lord and Master. This comes out very plainly in Jas. 1: 5, If any of you lacketh wisdom, let MM ask of God." It is clear that the promise is only made to believers. James does not say, "If any man lacketh wisdom, let him ask of God, but, If any of you lacketh wisdom, let him ask of God. There is no promise in the Word of God that God will guide anyone but the believer in Jesus Christ. Indeed there is no promise in the Word of God that He will answer the prayers of unbelievers about anything. God's guidance is the privilege of the believer in Jesus Christ and of him alone. By believer I do not mean the one who merely has an orthodox faith about Jesus Christ, but the one who is a believer in the Bible sense, that is, the one who has that living faith in Jesus Christ that leads him to receive Jesus Christ as his Lord and Savior, and to surrender his life to His service and control. If then, we would have God's sure guidance, the first thing to make sure of is that we really are believers, that we really are children of God, that we really have accepted Jesus Christ as our Savior, and really have surrendered our lives to His Lordship.

2. The second step toward obtaining God's guidance is that we clearly realize our own utter inability to decide for ourselves the way in which we should go. The promise, as we find it in the Word of God, makes this very plain. James says, "If any of you lacketh wisdom, let him ask of God, etc." The promise is made to the one who lacks wisdom, not the one who has it. It is made to the one who realizes the limitations of his own wisdom and realizes his dependence upon God for His wisdom. It is at this point that many, very many, fail of guidance. They have such confidence in their own opinions, in their own judgment, in their own ability to decide the course that they should pursue, that though they may as a formality ask God for His guidance, they do not really have any deep sense of their need of His guidance, and they have such confidence in their own wisdom that they mistake their own judgment for the guidance of God. Having prayed for Wisdom, but still being confident in their own judgment, they become all the more sure that their opinion is right and they attribute their own opinion to God. If we are to have God's guidance we must be utterly emptied of all confidence in our own judgment; and, in a sense of our own inability to decide for ourselves, we should come to God, putting our own notions utterly aside, for Him to tell us what He would have us to do, and we should wait silently before Him to make known His will.

3. The third step toward obtaining Divine guidance is that we really desire to know God's will, and are thoroughly willing to do it whatever it may be. This also comes out in the promise. It reads, "If any of you lacketh wisdom let him ask of God." Of course, the asking must be genuine, and there is no genuine asking wisdom of God unless we are eagerly desirous of knowing God's will and heartily willing to do it when that will is made known. The genuine and absolute surrender of the will to God is the great secret of guidance. The promise, "I will instruct thee and teach thee in the way which thou shalt go; I will counsel thee with mine eye upon thee, " as is evident from the context, is made to the one whose will is surrendered to God, for the next verse reads, "Be ye not as the horse, or as a mule, which have no understanding: whose trappings must be bit and bridle to hold them in, else they will not come unto thee." If we are mulish, that is if we are bent on doing our own will, then God must guide us with "bit and bridle," and oftentimes must break our jaw before we submit to Him. His instruction, teaching and guidance, His gentle guidance "with His eye upon us," is for the one whose will is entirely surrendered to Him. The surrender must be real surrender. There are many who think they wish to know and are willing to do God's will, and that it is God's will that they are waiting to know, but, what they are really seeking, is to get God to say yes to their own plans, and get God to endorse the plan they themselves have already subconsciously formed, and they are not waiting, as they suppose they are, until God tells them what His will really is, they are waiting until God tells them to do the thing that they want to do and, in their subconscious self, have made up their mind to do, so they think and think and think, and pray and pray and pray, until they think themselves into thinking that God tells them to do the thing that they themselves wished to do from the outset, and this thing that they wanted to do from the outset may not be God's plan at all. This is one of the most frequent causes of thinking we have the mind of God when we are only doing the thing that we want to do. Men and women who go to God for guidance in this way, i. e., without having absolutely put aside their own will and their own opinion, when they do think themselves into the place where they fancy that God has endorsed their plan, are the most positive in saying that "God tells me to do thus and so." So then, we must, if we would be guided of God, make absolutely sure that we have put away our own will entirely and are utterly willing to and desirous of doing God's will, whatever it may be.

We must be sure that we are silent before God and truly listening to His voice, and not still listening to this desire that we have in the depths of our heart that God shall tell us to do the thing that we want to do. When Mr. Moody invited me to take up the work in Chicago in 1889, I went to God to show me what might be His will. There was a great conflict in my heart. There were reasons why I wished to go to Chicago; there are reasons why I wished to stay in Minneapolis, or why I thought I must stay in Minneapolis. It took me three days to get absolutely silent before God, and to put away my own conflicting ideas on both sides. When I did come to the place where I had no will whatever in the matter, but simply wished to know what God's will was, whichever way it might be, when I became absolutely silent before God, God soon made the path in which He would have me go as plain as day.

The fact that the thing that we are contemplating doing is a hard thing, that it requires great sacrifice, does not by any means make it sure that it is God's will and not ours. Our hearts naturally are deceitful above all things, and oftentimes willful persons will set their heart on doing a very hard thing. They may set their heart upon doing it out of spiritual pride, or for many other reasons than because of surrender to the will of God. They want to do this hard thing, and they pray and pray and pray, and brood and brood and brood until they make themselves think that this hard thing is the will of God, when very likely the thing that God would have them do is some very humdrum, everyday sort of a thing. There is many a man and many a woman determined to be a foreign missionary, and a foreign missionary under the most difficult circumstances, whom God has called to a very quiet life at home, and while they are willing to endure the severest hardships in the foreign field, they are not willing to plod on quietly and unseen and unnoticed at home. But the best thing is God's will, whether that will be in a quiet humdrum life at home, or whether it be a notable life of courage and self-sacrifice in the foreign field; and, if we are to have God's guidance we must, as already said, become absolutely silent before God, and be willing and glad to serve Him in the most ordinary sort of life, a life that seems far beneath our talents and our training, if that be His will, just as ready to do that as to serve Him in a field that demands large abilities and great sacrifice. Satan cheats many of God's children out of accomplishing the things that God would have them do by making them restless in the homely paths that God opens up to them of doing things that they can do, and sets their heart upon doing things that they cannot do; and thus they leave the path of actual achievement to brood over things they would like to do, but which it is not God's will for them to do, and which they never will do. Oftentimes a whole life is spoiled in this way.

4. The fourth step toward obtaining God's guidance is definite prayer for that guidance. "If any of you lacketh wisdom," says God, "let him ask of God." There should be definite prayer for definite guidance. We should ask God's guidance at every turn of life; we should ask His guidance not merely in the great crises of life, but in the ordinary matters of everyday life, in our business, in our domestic work, in the most simple things. None of us knows enough to direct our own steps in the simplest matters of everyday life. We need God's guidance at every turn of life, and we can have it, and the way to get it is to ask for it. But the asking will do no good unless we have already taken the other steps that have been mentioned. The definite prayer is the fourth step and not the first, and we should be sure we have taken the first three steps before we take the fourth.

5. The fifth step toward obtaining God's guidance is positive expectation that God will grant our prayer and give us the guidance that we ask. This also comes out in the exact wording of the promise. It reads, "If any of you lack wisdom, let him ask of God, who giveth to all men liberally, and upbraideth not, and it shall be given him. But let him ask in faith, nothing doubting: for he that doubteth is like the surge of the sea driven by the wind and tossed. For let not that man (i.e., the man that doubts, the man who does not confidently expect) think that he shall receive anything of the Lord." Here is where many miss God's guidance. Their wills are surrendered, they really desire to know and do God's will, and they ask God for His guidance, but they do not confidently expect that God will give the guidance they ask. They hope He will, but they are not at all sure that He will. If we have taken the other steps, when we ask God for His guidance we may be absolutely sure that God will give it. Someone may say, "But others have asked God's guidance and thought they had it, when the event showed they did not. May not I also be mistaken?" No, not if you have taken the other steps already mentioned and will take the steps that we are still to mention. We have God's absolute promise of guidance made to those who meet the conditions which we have described, and therefore we may ask guidance with the absolute certainty that we are going to receive it. When we ask for God's wisdom, if we are of those to whom the promise is made, we know that we have asked something according to God's will, for He has definitely promised it in His Word, and, therefore, we have a right to know that our prayer is heard and the thing we have asked is granted.[3]

Some years ago, I was speaking at a Bible Conference of the Y. M. C. A. at White Bear Lake, Minn. I was speaking on the subject of prayer. As I left the platform to hurry to a train I found the next speaker waiting for me on the outside of the audience. He was greatly excited. He was a gifted teacher of the Word of God and had been much used of God. He stopped me as I passed by hurrying to the train and said, "I am going to tear to pieces everything you have said to these young men." I replied, "If I have not spoken according to the Book I hope you will tear it to pieces, but what did I say that was not according to the Bible?" He answered, "You have produced upon these young men the impression that we can ask things of God and get the very thing we ask." I replied, "I do not know whether that is the impression I produced or not, but that is certainly the impression that I meant to produce." "But," he said, "that is not right. We should pray, if it be Thy will." "Yes," I replied, "if we do

---

[3] *1 John 5:14, 15 -*

not know what the will of God is in the case we should say if it be Thy will, but if God has revealed His will in any specific instance why should we put in any if?" "But," he said, "we cannot know the will of God." "What is the Word of God given to us for," I asked, "if it is not to show us what the will of God is? For example, we are told in Jas. 1: 5-7, if any of you lacketh wisdom, let him ask of God, who giveth to all men liberally, and upbraideth not. Now," I said, "when you ask for wisdom do you not know by this specific promise that you have asked something according to the will of God, and that you are going to get it?" "But," he replied, "I do not know what wisdom is." I said, "If you knew what wisdom was, you would not need to ask for it, but whatever wisdom may be, do you not know that when you ask for wisdom God is going to give it?" He made no reply. What reply was there to make? Here we have a definite promise of God; and, if we meet the conditions of that promise, we may be, and ought to be, absolutely sure, that God will do as He says, absolutely sure that God will give us wisdom in this specific case in which we ask it. If we have any uncertainty at this point God will not give us the wisdom we ask. We should rest absolutely on God's plain promise, and when we ask for wisdom be absolutely sure that that wisdom is coming. How God gives wisdom we will consider later.

6. The sixth step toward obtaining God's guidance is to follow God's guidance a step at a time as He gives it. Here again is where many miss their way. Many seek to know the whole way before they take a single step, but God's method is to show us a step at a time. Look at Peter in Acts 12. God led him a step at a time: first the angel smote Peter on the side and awoke him, and told him to arise up quickly. This Peter did, and his chains fell from his hands. Then the angel said unto him, Gird thyself and bind on thy sandals," and he did so. Then the angel said, "Cast thy garment about thee, and follow me," and Peter did exactly as he was told. He was not even sure that he was awake, but he followed step by step, even when he thought he might be asleep. They passed the first and second guard and came to the iron gate that led into the city. Peter did not stop and argue as to whether the gate would be opened or not, but just followed up to the gate, and when he got to the gate the gate opened of its own accord. Thus God led him step by step, and thus God leads us. The Word of God tells us that "The steps of a good man are ordered of the Lord".[4] The trouble with many of us is we wish God to show us the whole path, and are not willing to go a step at a time. Look at Paul in the 16th chapter of the Acts of the Apostles, the 6th to 8th verses. Paul and his companions went through the region of Phrygia and Galatia and would have passed into the province of Asia to preach the Word there, but the Holy Ghost said, "No." So, Paul passed over against Hysia and was about to go into Bithynia, the next province. At that point "the Spirit of Jesus" again said, "No"; so passing by Mysia he came down to Troas, and there a vision appeared to Paul in the night, leading him to go over into Macedonia. Step by step the Spirit led, and step by step Paul followed on. The thing for us to do is to take the next step that God shows us in answer to our prayer and not wait until God shows us the whole way. A college student once came to me at the Northfield Students Convention, telling me that he was greatly perplexed as to his future life, that he had been asking God's guidance and could not get it. I asked Him what he was asking God's guidance about and he said, about what he should do when he got out of college. I said, "How far are you along in college?" and he said that the following fall he would begin his junior year. I said, "Then you have two years left in college. " "Yes." "Are you sure you ought to take those two years in college?" "Yes." "Then what you are perplexed about is because you cannot get guidance for two years from now." "Yes." " Well, just go on as God leads you, and in the two years if not before God will show you what to do next." A very large share of our perplexity about the will of God is of this kind. We are troubled because God has not shown us what He wants us to do next year, or it may be next month. All we need is God's guidance for to-day. Follow on step by step as He leads you and the way will open as you go.

7. There remains just one more step in the path that leads to God's sure guidance, and that is that we always bear in mind that God's guidance is clear guidance. Here is where many go astray. They have impulses, they know not from what source; they have what appear like leadings, for example, to go to the foreign field, or do some other thing, but they are not at all sure it is God's leading. Very likely it is not God's leading; and yet they follow it for fear they may be disobeying God, or, perhaps they do not follow it and then get into condemnation lest they

---

[4] *Ps. 37: 23 -*

have disobeyed God. I have met many in the deepest gloom from this cause. They had an impression they ought to do a certain thing, they were not at all clear the impression was from God, they did not do the thing, and then the devil has made them think that they have disobeyed God, and some even think they have committed the unpardonable sin because they did not obey this prompting (of the origin of which they were not at all sure). If we will only bear in mind that God's guidance is clear guidance we will be delivered from this snare of Satan. We are told in 1 John 1:5 that "God is light, and in Him is no darkness at all." Any leadings that are not absolutely clear, provided our wills are surrendered to God, are not from Him as yet. We have a right in every case where we have any impression that we ought to do a certain thing, but where we are not absolutely sure it is the will of God, to go to God and say to Him, "Heavenly Father, I desire to do Thy will; my will is absolutely surrendered to Thine, now if this is of Thee, make it clear as day and I will do it, and if our wills are absolutely surrendered to God and we fully realize our own inability to decide and are ready to be led by Him, God will make as clear as day if it is His will, and we have a right not to do it until He does make it clear, and we have a right to have an absolutely clear conscience in not doing it until He does make it clear. God is a Father and is more willing to make His will known to us than we are to make our will known to our children, provided we really wish to know and wish to do His will. We have no right to be in mortal dread before God and to be in constant apprehension that we have not done His will.

When we accepted Christ and surrendered our wills to God we did not receive the spirit of bondage again unto fear, but the Spirit that gives us the place as sons where we cry, "Abba, Father," in perfect childlike trust in Him.[5] We would not mislead our children in such a case, we would not leave our children to any doubts or uncertainty, we would make our will as clear as day, and so will God make His. Satan will prevent a man or woman making a full surrender to God just as long as he can, but when a man does make a full surrender, then the devil will do everything in his power to torment him. He will suggest all kinds of ridiculous things for him to do, and then the man will not do them and Satan will torment him by making him think he has gone back on his surrender to God. Let

---

[5] *Rom. 8:15 -*

us never forget that not all spiritual impressions are from the Holy Spirit. There are other spirits beside the Holy Spirit and we need to try the spirits whether they be of God (1 John 4:1). Some people are so anxious to be led of the Holy Spirit that they are willing to be led by any spirit and thus plunge into the delusions of spiritualism or "the tongues" business or other forms of fanaticism. I repeat it again: God's guidance is clear guidance and we should not follow any impression until God makes it as clear as day that it is from Him.

The main point in the whole matter of guidance is the absolute surrender of the will to God, the delighting in His will and the being willing to do joyfully the very things we would not like to do naturally, the very things in connection with which there may be many disagreeable circumstances because of association with or even subordination to people that we do not altogether like, and difficulties of other kinds, doing them joyfully simply because it is the will of God, and the willingness to let God lead in any way He pleases, whether it may be by His Word or by His Spirit. If we will only completely distrust our own judgment and have absolute confidence in God's judgment, and God's willingness to guide us, and are absolutely surrendered to His will, whatever it may be, and are willing to let God choose His way of guidance, and will go on step by step as He does guide us, and are studying His word to know His will, and are listening for the still small voice of the Spirit, going step by step as He leads, He will guide us with His eye. He will guide us with His counsel to the end of our earthly pilgrimage, and afterwards receive us into glory

How God Guides

Yet I am always with you;
you hold me by my right hand.
You guide me with your counsel,
and afterward you will take me into glory.[6]

T here are no promises in God's Word more precious to the man who wishes to do His will, and who realizes the goodness of His will, than the promises of God's guidance. What a cheering, gladdening, inspiring thought is that contained in the text, that we may have the guidance of infinite wisdom and love at every turn of life and that we have it to the end of our earthly pilgrimage.

There are few more precious words in the whole Book of Psalms, which is one of the most precious of all the books of the Bible, than these: "You hold me by my right hand. You guide me with your counsel, and afterward you will take me into glory." How the thoughtful and believing and obedient heart burns as it reads these wonderful words of the text! I wish we had time to dwell on the characteristics of God's guidance as they are set forth in so many places in the Word of God, but we must turn at once to consideration of the means God uses in guiding us.

I. God Guides by His Word

First of all, God guides by His Word. We read in Psalm 119:105, "Your word is a lamp to my feet and a light for my path," and in the 130th verse of this same Psalm we read, "The unfolding of your words gives light; it gives understanding to the simple." God's own written Word is the chief instrument that God uses in our guidance. God led the children of Israel by a pillar of cloud by day and a pillar of fire by night. The written Word, the Bible, is our pillar of cloud and pillar of fire. As it leads we follow. One of the main purposes of the Bible, the Word of God, is practical guidance in the affairs of everyday life. All other readings must be tested by the Word. Whatever promptings may come to us from

---

[6] *Psalm 73:23-24 -*

any other source, whether it be by human counsel or by the prompting of some invisible spirit, or in whatever way it may come, we must test the promptings, or the guidance or the counsel, by the sure Word of God, "To the law and to the testimony! If they do not speak according to this word, they have no light of dawn."[7]

Whatever spirit or impulse may move us, whatever dream or vision may come to us, or whatever apparently providential opening we may have, all must be tested by the Word of God. If the impulse or leading, or prompting, or vision, or providential opening is not according to the Book, it is not of God. "'Let the prophet who has a dream tell his dream, but let the one who has my word speak it faithfully. For what has straw to do with grain?' declares the LORD."[8] If Christians would only study the Word they would not be misled as they so often are by seducing spirits, or by impulses of any kind, that are not of God but of Satan or of their own deceitful hearts. How often people have said to me that the Spirit was leading them to do this or that, when the thing that they were being led to do was in direct contradiction to God's Word.

For example, a man once called on me to consult me about marrying a woman who he said was a beautiful Christian, that they had deep sympathy for the work of God, and that the Spirit of God was leading them to marry one another. "But," I said to the man, "you already have one wife." "Yes," he replied, "but you know we have not gotten along very well together." "Yes," I said, "I know that, and, furthermore, I have had a conversation with her and believe it is your fault more than hers. But, however that may be, if you should put her away and marry this other woman, Jesus Christ says that you would be an adulterer." "Oh, but," he replied, "the Spirit of God is leading us to one another." Now, whatever spirit may have been leading that man, it certainly was not the Spirit of God, for the Spirit of God cannot lead anyone to do that which is in direct contradiction to the Word of God. I replied to this man, "You are a liar and a blasphemer. How dare you attribute to the Spirit of God action that is directly contrary to the teaching of Jesus Christ?"

Many, many times Christian people have promptings from various sources which they attribute to the Holy Spirit, but which are in plain and flat contradiction to the clear and definite teachings of God's Word.

---

[7] *Isaiah 8:20 -*

[8] *Jeremiah 23:28 -*

The truth is, many so neglect the Word that they are all in a maze regarding the impulses and readings that come to them, as to where they come from; whereas, if they studied the Word they would at once detect the real character of these readings.

But the Word itself must be used in a right way if we are to find the leading of God from it. We have no right to seek guidance from the Word of God by using it in any fantastic way, as some do. For example, there is no warrant whatever in the Word of God for trying to find out God's will by opening the Bible at random and putting a finger on some text without regard to its real meaning as made clear by the context. There is no warrant whatever in the Bible for any such use of it. The Bible is not a talisman, or a fortune-telling book, it is not in any sense a magic book; it is a revelation from an infinitely wise God, made in a reasonable way, to reasonable beings, and we obtain God's guidance from the Bible by taking the verse of Scripture in which the guidance is found, in the connection in which it is found in the Bible, and interpreting it, led by the Holy Spirit, in its context as found in the Bible. Many have fallen into all kinds of fanaticism by using their Bible in this irrational and fantastic way.

Some years ago, a prediction was made by a somewhat prominent woman Bible teacher that on a certain date Oakland and Alameda and some other California cities, and I think also Chicago, were to be swallowed up in an earthquake. The definite date was set and many were in anticipation, and many in great dread. A friend of mine living in Chicago was somewhat disturbed over the matter and sought God's guidance by opening her Bible at random, and this was the passage to which she opened:

The word of the LORD came to me: "Son of man, tremble as you eat your food, and shudder in fear as you drink your water. Say to the people of the land: 'This is what the Sovereign LORD says about those living in Jerusalem and in the land of Israel: They will eat their food in anxiety and drink their water in despair, for their land will be stripped of everything in it because of the violence of all who live there. The inhabited towns will be laid waste and the land will be desolate. Then you will know that I am the LORD.'" The word of the LORD came to me: "Son of man, what is this proverb you have in the land of Israel: 'The days go by and every vision comes to nothing'? Say to them, 'This is what the Sovereign LORD says: I am going to put an end to this proverb, and they will no longer quote it in Israel.' Say to them, 'The days are near when every vision will be fulfilled. For there will be no more false visions or flattering divinations among the people of Israel. But I the LORD will speak what I will, and it shall be fulfilled without delay. For in your days, you rebellious house, I will fulfill whatever I say, declares the Sovereign LORD.'" The word of the LORD came to me: "Son of man, the house of Israel is saying, 'The vision he sees is for many years from now, and he prophesies about the distant future.'" Therefore, say to them, "This is what the Sovereign LORD says: 'None of my words will be delayed any longer; whatever I say will be fulfilled, declares the Sovereign LORD.'"[9]

Of course, this seemed like a direct answer, and, if it were a direct answer, it clearly meant that the prophecy of the destruction of Oakland, Alameda, and Chicago would be fulfilled at once, on the day predicted. The woman told me of this that very day, but I was not at all disturbed. As we all know, the prophecy was not fulfilled, and this would-be prophetess sank out of sight, and, so far as I know, has not been heard from since. Many years afterward an earthquake did come to San Francisco and work great destruction, but San Francisco was not in this woman's prophecy, and Oakland and Alameda were, and they were left practically untouched by the earthquake, and certainly did not sink out of sight as the woman had predicted. And, furthermore, the earthquake that came to an adjoining city was many years after the prophesied date. This is only one illustration among many that might be given of how utterly misleading is any guidance that we get in this fantastic and unwarranted way.

Furthermore, the fact that some text of Scripture comes into your mind at some time when you are trying to discover God's will is not by any means proof positive that it is just the Scripture for you at that time. The devil can suggest Scripture. He did this in tempting our Lord,[10] and he does it today. If the text suggested, taken in its real meaning as determined by the language used and by the context, applies to your present position, it is, of course, a message from God for you, but the mere fact that a text of Scripture comes to mind at some time, which by a distortion from its proper meaning might apply to our case, is no evidence

---

[9] *Ezekiel 12:17-28 -*
[10] *Matthew 4:6 -*

whatever that it is the guidance of God. May I repeat once more than in getting guidance from God's Word we must take the words as they are found in their context, and interpret them according to the proper meaning of the words used and apply them to those to whom it is evident from the context that they were intended to apply. But with this word of warning against seeking God's guidance from the Word of God in fantastic and unwarranted ways, let me repeat that God's principal way of guiding us, and the way by which all other methods must be tested, is by His written Word.

II. God Leads by His Spirit

God also leads us by His Spirit, that is, by the direct leading of the Spirit in the individual heart. Beyond question, there is such a thing as an "inner light." We read in Acts 8:29, "The Spirit told Philip, 'Go to that chariot and stay near it.'" In a similar way, we read in Acts 16:6-7, of the Apostle Paul and his companions: "Paul and his companions traveled throughout the region of Phrygia and Galatia, having been kept by the Holy Spirit from preaching the word in the province of Asia. When they came to the border of Mysia,[11] they tried to enter Bithynia, but the Spirit of Jesus would not allow them to." In one of these passages we see God by His Holy Spirit giving direct personal guidance to Philip as to what he should do, and in the other passage we see the Spirit restraining Paul and his companions from doing something they otherwise would have done. There is no reason why God should not lead us as directly as He led Philip and Paul in their day, and those who walk near God can testify that He does so lead.

I was once walking on South Clark Street, Chicago, near the corner of Adams, a very busy corner. I had passed by hundreds of people as I walked. Suddenly I met a man, a perfect stranger, and it seemed to me as if the Spirit of God said to me, "Speak to that man." I stopped a moment and stepped into a doorway and asked God to show me if the guidance was really from Him. It became instantly clear that it was. I turned around and followed the man, who had reached the corner and was crossing from one side of Clark Street to the other. I caught up to him in the in middle of the street. Providentially, for a moment there was

---

[11] Mysia *was a region in the northwest of ancient Asia Minor (Anatolia, Asian part of modern Turkey) -*

no traffic at that point. Even on that busy street we were alone in the middle of the street. I laid my hand on his shoulder as we crossed to the farther sidewalk, and said to him, "Are you a Christian?" He replied, "That is a strange thing to ask a perfect stranger on the street." I said, "I know it is, and I do not ask every man that I meet on the street that question, but I believe God told me to ask you." He stopped and hung his head. He said, "This is very strange. I am a graduate of Amherst College, but I am a perfect wreck through drink here in Chicago, and only yesterday my cousin, who is a minister in this city, was speaking to me about my soul, and for you, a perfect stranger, to put this question to me here on this busy street" I did not succeed in bringing the man to a decision there on the street, but shortly afterward he was led to a definite acceptance of Christ.

A friend of mine walking the busy streets of Toronto suddenly had a deep impression that he should go to the hospital and speak to someone there. He tried to think of someone he knew at the hospital and he could think of but one man. He took it for granted that he was the man he was to speak to, but when he reached the hospital and came to this man's bedside there was no reason why he should speak to him, and nothing came of the conversation. He was in great perplexity, and standing by his friend's bed he asked God to guide him. He saw a man lying on the bed right across the aisle. This man was a stranger, he had been brought to the hospital for an apparently minor trouble, some difficulty with his knee. His case did not seem at all urgent, but my friend turned and spoke to him and had the joy of leading him to Christ. To everybody's surprise, that man passed into eternity that very night. It was then or never.

So, God often guides us today (if we are near Him and listening for His guidance), leading us to do things that otherwise we would not do, and restraining us from doing things we otherwise would do. But these inward readings must be always tested by the Word, and we do well when any prompting comes to look up to God and ask Him to make clear to us if this leading is of Him, otherwise we may be led to do things which are absurd and not at all according to the will of God.

But though it is oftentimes our privilege to be thus led by the Spirit of God, there is no warrant whatever in the Word of God for our refusing to act until we are thus led. Remember, this is not God's only method of guidance. Oftentimes we do not need this particular kind of guidance.

Take the cases of Philip and of Paul to which we have referred. God did not guide Philip and Paul in this way in every step they took. Philip had done many things in coming down through Samaria to the desert where he met the treasurer of Queen Candace, and it was not until the chariot of the treasurer appeared that God led Philip directly by His Spirit. And so with Paul, who in the missionary work to which God had called him had followed his own best judgment as God enlightened it until the moment came when he needed the special direct prohibition of the Holy Spirit of his going into a place where God would not have him go at that time.

There is no need for our having the Spirit's direction to do that which the Spirit has already told us to do in the Word. For example, many a man who has fanatical and unscriptural notions about the guidance of the Holy Spirit refuses to work in an after-meeting because, as he says, the Holy Spirit does not lead him to speak to anyone, and he is waiting until the Holy Spirit does. But as the Word of God plainly teaches him to be a fisher of men (Matthew 4:19; 28:19; Acts 8:4), if he is to obey God's word, whenever there is opportunity to work with men he should go to work, and there is no need of the Holy Spirit's special guidance. Paul would have gone into these places to preach the Gospel if the Holy Spirit had not forbidden him. He would not have waited for some direct command of the Spirit to preach, and when we have an opportunity to speak to lost souls we should speak, unless restrained. What we need is not some direct impulse of the Holy Spirit to make us speak, the Word already commands us to do that; what we need, if we are not to speak, is that the Spirit should directly forbid us to speak.

Furthermore, let me repeat again what we should bear in mind about the Spirit's guidance, that He will not lead us to do anything that is contrary to the Word of God. The Word of God is the Holy Spirit's book, and He never contradicts His own teaching. Many people do things that are strictly forbidden in the Word of God, and justify themselves in so doing by saying the Spirit of God guides them to do it; but any spirit that guides us to do something that is contrary to the Holy Spirit's own book cannot by any possibility be the Holy Spirit.

For example, some time ago, in reasoning with one of the leaders of the Tongues Movement about the utterly unscriptural character of their assemblies, I called his attention to the fact that in the 14th chapter of

1st Corinthians we have God's explicit command that not more than two, or, at the most, three, persons should be allowed to speak "in a tongue" in any one meeting, and that the two or three that did speak must not speak at the same time, but "in turn," and if there were no interpreter present, not even one should be allowed to speak in a tongue, that (while he might speak in private with himself in a tongue, even with no interpreter present) he must "keep silent in the church." I called this man's attention to the fact that in their assembly they disobeyed every one of these three things that God commanded. He defended himself and his companions by saying, "But we are led by the Spirit of God to do these things, and therefore are not subject to the Word." I called his attention to the fact that the Word of God in this passage was given by the Holy Spirit for the specific purpose of guiding the assembly in its conduct and that any spirit that led them to disobey these explicit commandments of the Holy Spirit Himself, given through His Apostle Paul and recorded in His Word, could not by any possibility be the Holy Spirit. Here, again, we should always bear in mind that there are spirits other than the Holy Spirit, and we should "test the spirits to see whether they are of God," and we should try them by the Word. One of the gravest mistakes that anyone can make in his Christian life is that of being so anxious for spirit guidance that he is willing to open his soul to any spirit who may come along and try to lead him.

Furthermore, we should always bear in mind that there is absolutely no warrant in the Word of God for supposing that the Holy Spirit leads into strange and absurd ways, or does strange and absurd things. For example, some have certain signs by which they discern, as they say, the Holy Spirit's guidance. For example, some look for a peculiar twitching of the face, or for some other physical impulse. With some the test is a shudder, or cold sensation down the back. When this comes they take it as clear evidence that the Holy Spirit is present. In a former day, and to a certain extent today, some judge the Spirit's presence by what they call "the jerks," that is, a peculiar jerking that takes possession of a person, which they supposed to be the work of the Holy Spirit. All this is absolutely unwarranted by the Word of God and dishonoring to the Holy Spirit. We are told distinctly and emphatically in 2 Timothy 1:7 that the Holy Spirit is a spirit "of power, of love and of self-discipline." The word translated "self-discipline" really means "sound sense," and, therefore, any spirit that leads us to do ridiculous things, cannot be the Holy Spirit.

There are some who defend the most outrageous improprieties and even indecencies in public assemblies, saying that the Holy Spirit prompts them to these things. By this claim they make flies directly in the face of God's own Word, which teaches us specifically in 1 Corinthians 14:32-33 "The spirits of prophets are subject to the control of prophets. For God is not a God of disorder but of peace." And in the 40th verse we are told that "everything" in a Spirit-governed assembly should be "done in a fitting and orderly way." The word translated "fitting" in this passage means "in a becoming [or respectable] way," which certainly does not permit the disorders and immodesties, and confusions and indecencies and absurdities that occur in many assemblies that claim to be Spirit led, but which, tested by the Word of God, certainly are not led by the Holy Spirit.

III. God Guides Us by Enlightening Our Judgment

In the third place, God guides us by enlightening our judgment. We see an illustration of this in the case of the Apostle Paul in Acts 16:10. God had been guiding Paul by a direct impression produced in his heart by the Holy Spirit, keeping him from going to certain places which otherwise he would have gone. Then God gives to Paul in the night a vision, and, having received the vision, Paul, by his own enlightened judgment, concludes from it what God has called him to do. This is God's ordinary method of guidance when His Word does not specifically tell us what to do. We go to God for wisdom, we make sure that our wills are completely surrendered to Him, and that we realize our dependence on Him for guidance, then God clears up our judgment and makes it clear to us what we should do. Here again we should always bear in mind that "God is light and in him is no darkness at all," and that, therefore, God's guidance is clear guidance, and we should not act until things are made perfectly plain.

Many miss God's guidance by doing things too soon. Had they waited until God had enabled them to see clearly, under the illumination of His Holy Spirit, they would have avoided disastrous mistakes. The principle that "the one who trusts will never be dismayed," (Isaiah 28:16) applies right here. On the other hand, when any duty is made clear we should do it at once. If we hesitate to act when the way is made clear, then we soon get into doubt and perplexity and are all confused as to what God would have us do. Many, many a man has seen the path of duty as clear as day before him, and, instead of stepping out at once, has hesitated even when the will of God has become perfectly clear, and before long was plunged into absolute uncertainty as to what God would have him do.

IV. God May Guide by Visions and Dreams

In Acts 16:9-10, we are told how God guided Paul by a vision, and there are other instances of such guidance, not only before Pentecost, but after. God may so guide people today. However, that was not God's usual method of guiding men, even in Bible times, and it is even less His usual way since the giving of His Word and the giving of the Holy Spirit. We do not need that mode of guidance as the Old Testament saints needed it, for we now have the complete Word and we also have the Spirit in a sense and in a fullness that the Old Testament saints did not have. God does lead by dreams today.

When I was a boy, sleeping in a room in our old home in Geneva, N. Y., I dreamed I was sleeping in that room and that my mother, who I dreamed was dead (though she was really living at the time) came and stood by my bed, with a face like an angel's, and begged me to enter the ministry, and in my sleep I promised her that I would. In a few moments I awoke and found it all a dream, but I never could get away from that promise. I never had rest in my soul until I did give up my plans for life and promise God that I would preach.

But the matter of dreams is one in which we should exercise the utmost care, and we should be very careful and prayerful and Scriptural in deciding that any dream is from God. Only the other day a brilliant and highly educated woman called at my office to tell me some wonderful dreams that she had and what these dreams proved. Her interpretation of the dreams was most extraordinary and fantastic. But while dreams are a very uncertain method of guidance, it will not do for us to say that God never so guides, but it is the height of folly to seek God's guidance in that way, and especially to dictate that God shall guide in that way.

V. God Does Not Guide by Casting Lots in This Dispensation

In Acts 1:24-26 we learn that the apostles sought guidance in choosing by lot one to take the place of Judas. This method of finding God's will was common in the Old Testament times, but it belongs entirely to the old dispensation. This is the last case on record. It was never used after Pentecost. We need today no such crude way of ascertaining the will of God, as we have the Word and the Spirit at our disposal. Neither should we seek signs. That belongs to the imperfect dispensation that is past, and even then it was a sign of unbelief.

VI. God Guides by His Providence

God has still another way of guiding us besides those already mentioned, and that is by His providences, that is, He so shapes the events of our lives that it becomes clear that He would have us go in a certain direction or do a certain thing. For example, God puts an unsaved man directly in our way so that we are alone with him and thus have an opportunity for conversation with him. In such a case we need no vision to tell us, and we need no mighty impulse of the Holy Spirit to tell us, that we ought to speak to this man about his soul. The very fact that we are alone with him and have an opportunity for conversation is of itself all the Divine guidance we need. We do need, however, to look to God to tell us what to say to him and how to say it, but God will not tell us by some supernatural revelation what to say, but by making clear to our own minds what we should say.

In a similar way, if a man needs work to support himself or family, and a position for honest employment opens to him, he needs no inner voice, no direct leading of the Holy Spirit, to tell him to take the work; the opening opportunity is of itself God's guidance by God's providence.

We must, however, be very careful and very prayerful in interpreting "the readings of providence." What some people call "the leading of providence" means no more than the easiest way. When Jonah was fleeing from God and went down to Joppa he found a ship just ready to start for Tarshish (Jonah 1:3). If he had been like many today he would have interpreted that as meaning it was God's will that he should go to Tarshish, as there was a ship Just starting for Tarshish, instead of to Nineveh, to which city God had commanded him to go. In point of fact, Jonah did take the ship to Tarshish but he "was under no illusion in the matter, he knew perfectly well that he was not going where God wanted him to go, and he got into trouble for it. Oftentimes people seek guidance by providence by asking God to shut up a certain way that is opening to them, if it is not His will that they should go that way. There is no warrant whatever for doing that. God has given us our judgment and is ready to illuminate our judgment, and we have no right to act the part of children and to ask Him to shut up the way so we cannot possibly go that way if it is not His will.

Some fancy that the easy way is necessarily God's way, but oftentimes the hard way is God's way. Our Lord Himself said, as recorded in Matthew 16:24, "If anyone would come after me, he must deny himself and take up his cross and follow me." That certainly is not the easy way. There are many who advise us to "follow the path of least resistance," but the path of least resistance is not always God's way by any means.

Some ask God to guide them providentially by removing all difficulties from the path in which He would have them go, but we have no right to offer such a prayer. God wishes us to be men and women of character and to surmount difficulties, and oftentimes He will allow difficulties to pile up in the very way in which we ought to go, and the fact that we see that a path is full of difficulties is no reason for deciding it is not the way God would have us go. Nevertheless, God does guide us by His providence, and we have no right to despise His providential guidance. For example, one may desire to go to China or to Africa as a missionary, and God does not give him the health requisite for going to China or to Africa. He should take that as clear providential guidance that he ought not to go, and seek some other opportunity for serving God.

Many people are asking God to open some door of opportunity, and God does open a door of opportunity right away, but it is not the kind of work they would especially like to do, so they decline to see in it a door of opportunity. The whole difficulty is that they are not wholly surrendered to the will of God.

Before we close this subject let us repeat again what cannot be emphasized too much or too often, that all readings, whether they be by the Spirit, by visions, by providences, by our own judgment, or by advice of friends, or in any other way, must be tested by the Word of God.

The main point in the whole matter of guidance is absolute surrender of the will to God, delighting in His will, and willingness to do joyfully the very things we would not like to do naturally, the very things in connection with which there may be many disagreeable circumstances, because, for example, of association with, or even subordination to, those that we do not altogether like, or difficulties of other kinds. It is to do joyfully what we are to do, simply because it is the will of God, and the willingness to let God lead in any way He pleases, whether it be by His Word, or His Spirit, or by the enlightening of our judgment, or by His providence, or by whatever way He will. If only we will completely distrust our own judgment and have absolute confidence in God's judgment and God's willingness to guide us, and are absolutely surrendered to His will, whatever it may be, and are willing to let God choose His way of guidance, and will go on step by step as He does guide us, and if we are daily studying His Word to know His will, and are listening for the still small voice of the Spirit, going step by step as He leads, He will guide us with His eye; He will guide us with His counsel to the end of our earthly pilgrimage, and afterward receive us into glory.

How *to be*
Inexpressibly Happy

I have here a beautiful text, a text that you all know, but I wonder how many of you have ever pondered it enough to take in all its wonderful wealth of meaning.

A young woman in England many years ago always wore a golden locket that she would not allow anyone to open or look into, and everyone thought there must be some romance connected with that locket and that in that locket must be the picture of the one she loved. The young woman died at an early age, and after her death the locket was opened, everyone wondering whose face he would find within. And in the locket was found simply a little slip of paper with these words written upon it, "Though I have not seen Him, I love." Her Lord Jesus was the only lover she knew and the only lover she longed for, and she had gone to be with Him, the one object of her whole heart's devotion, the unseen but beloved Savior.

But it is to the last part of the verse that I wish to call your particular attention tonight, "Even though you do not see him now, you believe in him and are filled with an inexpressible and glorious joy."

This text informs us (and many of us do not need to be informed of it, for we know it by blessed experience) that one who really believes on Jesus Christ, our unseen, but ever living Lord and Savior, rejoices with "inexpressible and glorious joy." The Greek word translated "joy" is a very strong word, describing extreme joy or jubilant joy. The word "inexpressible" declares that this jubilant joy is of such a character that we cannot, by any possibility, explain it adequately to others. Everyone who really believes on the Lord Jesus does rejoice with a jubilant joy that is beyond all description. And those who do truly believe on the Lord Jesus Christ are the only ones who rejoice this way. Others may have a certain amount of joy, a certain measure of gladness, but the only people who really know "inexpressible and glorious joy" are those who really believe on Jesus Christ.

Who is there among us who does not wish to be happy? Happiness is the one thing all men are seeking. One man seeks it in one way, and another man seeks it in another way, but all men are in pursuit of it. Even the man who is "happy only when he is miserable" is seeking happiness in this strange way of cultivating a delightful melancholy by always looking on the dark side of things. One man seeks money because he thinks that money will make a man happy. Another man seeks worldly pleasure because he thinks that worldly pleasure will make a man happy. Still another seeks learning, the knowledge of science, or philosophy, or history, or literature, because he thinks that learning brings the true joy; but they are all in pursuit of the one thing, happiness.

The vast majority of men who seek happiness do not find it. You may say what you please, but for the majority of men this is an unhappy world. I go down into the houses of the poor, I do not find many happy people there. I go into the homes of the rich, I do not find many happy people even there. Study the faces of the people you meet on the street, at places of entertainment, or anywhere else, how many really radiant faces do you see? When you do see one it is so exceptional that you note it at once. But there is a way, and a very simple way, a very sure way, and a way that is open to all, not only to find happiness, but to be unspeakably happy. Our text tells us what that way is. Listen, "Even though you do not see him now, you believe in him and are filled with an inexpressible and glorious joy."

This statement of Peter's is true. How do I know it is true? In the first place, I know it is true because the Word of God says so. Whatever this book says is true. In the second place, I know it is true because I have put the matter to the test of personal experience and found it true. A good many people say, "I do not believe the Bible." Well, I do. I believe the Bible for a good many sufficient reasons; but there is this one reason why I believe the Bible that I wish to mention tonight: I believe the Bible because I have personally tested scores and scores of its most astonishing and apparently most incredible statements and found every one of them true in my own experience. Don't you think that if I knew a man who made very many statements that I could test for myself, some of them apparently incredible, and I tested these statements one after another through a long period of years, and found every one of them true, and never one single statement failed, don't you think that I would believe that man after a while? Well, that is just my experience with the Bible, and I believe it. I would be a fool if I did not. The statement of the text is one of those that I have tested, and I have found it true.

I was not always happy. Indeed, I was once unspeakably miserable. I had sought happiness very earnestly. I had sought happiness in amusement and sin, and found, not joy, but wretchedness. In my pursuit of happiness, I had tried study, the study of languages, science, philosophy and literature, but I did not find happiness in these things. At last I turned to Jesus Christ and believed on Him, and I found not merely happiness, but something better, joy, "inexpressible and glorious joy." Whatever heaven may be or may not be, I know that on this earth he who really believes on Jesus Christ, who puts himself in Christ's hands, to be led, and taught, and guided, and strengthened, puts himself in the hands of Jesus Christ for Jesus Christ to do all He will with him, I know that such a person finds "inexpressible and glorious joy."

Why Those Who Believe *in* Jesus Christ
Have Inexpressible *and* Glorious Joy

First of all, those who believe on Jesus Christ have "inexpressible and glorious joy" because they know that their sins are all forgiven. It is a wonderful thing to know that your sins are all forgiven, to know that there is not one single, slightest cloud between you and God, to know that no matter how many, or how great your sins may have been, that they are all blotted out; to know that God has put them all behind His back, where no one can ever get at them; to know that God has sunk all your sins in the depths of the sea, from which they can never be raised; that they are all gone. A little boy once asked his mother, "Mother, where are our sins after they are blotted out?" His mother replied, "My boy, where are those figures that you erased from your paper yesterday?" He answered, "I rubbed them out." Then she asked, "Where are they now?" he replied, "They are nowhere." "Well," she said, "that is just the same with your sins when God has blotted them out. They are nowhere. They have ceased to be."

Oh, friends, what a joy it is to know that there is not one single tiny cloud between you and the Holy God whom we call Father and who rules this universe. Suppose that you had offended the laws of the nation and had been sent to prison on a life sentence, and a pardon were brought to you, do you not think you would be happy? But that is nothing compared with the joy of knowing that your every sin is blotted out. Some years ago, Governor Stuart of Pennsylvania determined to pardon one of the prisoners in the Pennsylvania State prison, so he sent for Mr. Moody and said to him, "I have determined to pardon one of the prisoners in our state's prison, and I want you to go and take the pardon to him. You can preach to the prisoners if you want to while you are doing it." So, Mr. Moody went, carrying the pardon with him, and before he began to preach he said, "I have a pardon for one of you men that the Governor has sent by me." He did not intend to tell who it was who was pardoned until the sermon was over, but as he looked around on his audience and saw how anxious they all were, how eager they were, how a very agony of suspense was in their faces, Mr. Moody thought, "This will never do, I can't keep these men in this suspense," so he said, "I will tell you now who the man is," and he read his name from the pardon. Do you not think that, that was a glad moment for that one man out of those hundreds of prisoners, a glad moment for the one man who had the Governor's pardon, and who could walk out of prison a free man? Yes, but that is nothing to knowing that the eternal God has eternally pardoned your sins. Every true Christian knows that, he knows that every one of his sins is forgiven. How does he know it? Because the Bible says so in many places.

For example, it says in Acts 13:39, "And by him all that believe are justified from all things, from which ye could not be justified by the law of Moses," so we know it because God says so. But no one but the believer in Jesus Christ knows that his sins are all forgiven. If anyone who is not a believer in Jesus Christ says, "I know my sins are all forgiven," he says what is not true; for he does not know it, and cannot know it, for it is not a fact; but a Christian knows it because the Word of God says so.

The Christian knows his sins are all forgiven for another reason, that is, because the Holy Spirit bears witness in his own heart to the fact. One day, when the Apostle Peter was preaching to Cornelius, the Roman officer, and to his household, he said, "To him give all the prophets witness, that through his name whosoever believeth in him shall receive remission of sins,"[12] and everyone in his audience believed it. The Spirit

---

[12] *Acts 10:43 -*

of God descended right then and there and filled their hearts with the knowledge of sins forgiven, and they "began to magnify God" with jubilant hearts and jubilant voices. I tell you that was a joyful meeting.

A king, a great king, once wrote one of the greatest songs that ever was written. That song has lasted through the ages. It has been sung and is still being sung by thousands. It has been sung by millions, and though it was written many centuries ago, it is just as sweet today as the day the king wrote it. The man who wrote this song was a great king, the greatest king of his day, he was also one of the greatest generals of his day, one of the greatest generals of any day. He had great armies, the all-conquering armies of the day. He had a magnificent palace. I do not suppose that any other earthly king was ever so beloved as he was. His song was about joy and about happiness. He does not say in that song, "How happy is the man who is a great king," or, "How happy is the man who is a great general." What does he say? "Blessed is he whose transgressions are forgiven, whose sins are covered"[13]: "There is no happiness like the joy of knowing your sins are all forgiven." Oh, what a joy thrills the heart when a man knows that his sins are fully, freely, and forever forgiven. That is one reason why he who believes on Jesus Christ is inexpressibly happy, and you can have that inexpressible happiness today. I do not care how black your life may have been in the past; I do not care how far you may have wandered from God; I do not care how old you may have grown in sin; if you take Jesus Christ today for your Savior and your Lord, and believe on Him, your every sin will be blotted out, and it will be your privilege to know it.

In the second place, those who believe on Jesus Christ rejoice with "inexpressible and glorious joy" because they are free from the most grinding and crushing of all forms of slavery, the slavery of sin. There is many a slave in this audience tonight. Some of you are slaves of strong drink. Some of you men and some of you women are slaves of drink. You know you are slaves of drink. Some of you are slaves of drugs. Some of you are slaves of an uncontrollable temper. Some of you are slaves of acts of impurity or impurity of thought. Some of you are slaves of other sins. The grossest, vilest, most degrading slavery in the universe is the slavery of sin. Yes, many of you here tonight are slaves. But the Lord Jesus says

---

[13] *Psalm 32:1 -*

in John 8:31, 32, " If ye continue in my word, then are ye my disciples indeed; And ye shall know the truth, and the truth shall make you free." He says again in the thirty-sixth verse, "If the Son therefore shall make you free, ye shall be free indeed." There is not a slave in this building tonight who cannot have his chains snapped in a moment, yes, in a moment, by the mighty Son of God, if only he will believe on Jesus and trust Him to do it. How many a man and how many a woman I have known who once were slaves of sin in its most degrading and hopeless forms, who now are free.

One of the dearest and most honored and most useful friends I ever had was Sam Hadley of New York City. Sam Hadley was once hopelessly enslaved by sin. Strong drink had utterly mastered him and undermined his character. He had committed 138 forgeries and was being sought for by the police. One night, after having spent the night before in a New York jail with the "shakes," in a mission meeting a few blocks away from the jail he cried to Jesus to save him, and Jesus saved him right then and there; and I have often heard him say that never from that night had he ever had the slightest desire for that which had enslaved him more than anything else, intoxicating drink. My, what a happy man he became! All who knew him testified that he had "inexpressible and glorious joy." I wish you could have looked in Sam Hadley's face and seen the joy in that redeemed and radiant countenance. But we do not need to call Sam Hadley back from heaven to testify, for there are hundreds of people right here in this building tonight who once were complete slaves, who now are God's free men and free women, and who could testify to the fact. That is one reason why we are inexpressibly happy, because we are free. How the Southern Blacks rejoiced when they came to understand they were set free. They shouted and sang, "Glory! Glory! Hallelujah!" Why? Because once they were slaves, but now were free. No wonder, then, that we rejoice with "inexpressible and glorious joy" because we know that we are free, and free forever.

In the third place, those who believe on Jesus Christ rejoice with "inexpressible and glorious joy," because they are delivered from all fear. There is nothing that darkens the human heart more and robs it of all joy and fills it with gloom than fear in some of its many forms.

Those who truly believe on Jesus Christ are saved from all fear. They are delivered from all fear of misfortune; they are delivered from all fear of man; they are delivered from all fear of death; they are delivered from all fear of eternity. Do you know, friends, that to a true believer in Jesus Christ "eternity" is one of the sweetest words in the English language? Oh, how it makes our hearts swell, that word, "eternity." But "eternity" is not a sweet word to the unsaved. Write these words, "Where will you spend eternity?" on a card and hand it to a man who is not a Christian, and they will make him mad; write these same words, "Where will you spend eternity?" on a card and hand it to a Christian, and they will make him glad. Why is it? Simply because a true believer on Jesus Christ is not afraid of but delights in thoughts of eternity. Why, to him who believes on Jesus Christ eternity is glory.

In the fourth place, he who believes on Jesus Christ rejoices with "inexpressible and glorious joy" because he knows he will live forever. Is not that something to rejoice over? Is it not wonderful? We read in 1 John 2:17, "And the world passeth away, and the lust thereof: but he that doeth the will of God abideth forever. We all know that it is true that "the world passes away." We certainly ought to know it by this time; but it is equally true that "he who does the will of God lives forever."

Sometimes as we ride along our beautiful roads we see the stately mansions of our multimillionaires, and one will think, "It must be very pleasant to live there." Well, I suppose it must be, but think a moment. How long will these people live there? Perhaps the father of the household may live there ten years, possibly twenty years. Then where does he live? Some of the children may live there twenty, thirty, possibly, forty years, then what? The grave. I tell you it is not worth much after all. But the Christian looks on, and on, and on, to a life that has no end, to a life that is eternal. Glory!

In the fifth place, those who truly believe on Jesus Christ rejoice greatly with "inexpressible and glorious joy" because they know they are children of God. It is a great thing to know that you are a child of God. How does the Christian know it? He knows it because God says so in John 1:12, "But as many as received him, to them gave the power to become the sons of God, even to them that believe on his name:" A child of God, think of it! Sometimes as I have traveled around the world someone would point out to me some man, and say, "That man is the son of such and such a man, naming some king. Would you not like to be the son of a great king? Just look at that young man. He is the son of a king." In one country many years ago, when the king business was better than it is today, I was taken up and introduced to the son of one of the reigning monarchs of Europe, and the man who introduced me whispered to me, "He is the son of So-and-So" (naming the king). Well, what of it? He was a fine man in himself, but what if he was the son of a king? I am a son of God, and that is far greater, and every believer in Jesus Christ in this building tonight is a child of God, the child of "the King of kings." And any one of you here tonight, if you are not already a child of God, can become one in an instant by receiving the Lord Jesus.

In the sixth place, and very closely connected with the last, true believers in Jesus Christ rejoice with "inexpressible and glorious joy" because they are heirs of God, and joint-heirs with Jesus Christ. Is that not wonderful? We are so familiar with it we do not stop to take in the meaning of it. One of England's dukes lay dying. He called his brother to him, the one who would succeed to the title, and said, "Brother, in a few hours now you will be a duke and I will be a king." He was already a child of the King and in a few hours he himself would be a king. I, too, will be a king in a few days. You may say, "It may be many years." Well, many years are only a few days on the scale of eternity. And, if you really are a believer in Christ Jesus, if you have a real living faith in Him, you, too, will be a king in a few days.

There was never a royal pageant sweeping through the streets of London at any coronation comparable in glory to the glory that awaits you and me just over yonder. "When Christ, who is our life, shall appear, then shall ye also appear with him in glory.[14] We may be poor today. That does not matter. This life will be over in a moment and the other life begun, and that life is eternal.

In the seventh place, those who truly believe on Jesus Christ, those who throw their hearts wide open to Him, is those who surrender absolutely to Him, rejoice with "inexpressible and glorious joy" because God gives them the Holy Spirit, and there is no other joy in the present life like the joy of the Holy Spirit. One Monday morning, in Chicago, my front doorbell rang. I kept Monday in those days for my rest day, and had a notice above the doorbell, "Mr. Torrey does not see anyone on Monday." The maid went to the door, and there stood a poor woman. The

---

[14] *Colossians 3:4 -*

maid said, "Mr. Torrey does not see anyone on Monday. Did you not see the notice over the doorbell?" She said, "I knew that, but I have got to see him and you just go and tell him a member of his church must see him." So, the maid brought her into the reception room. She was a washerwoman. The maid showed the washerwoman a seat and came upstairs and said to me, "There is a woman downstairs who is a member of your church and says she has got to see you." So down I went.

As I entered the room she arose and hurried toward me, and said, "Mr. Torrey, I knew you did not see anybody on Monday, but I had to see you. Last night after I went to bed I was filled with the Holy Spirit right there in my bed, and I was so happy I could not sleep all night, and this morning I had to come and tell somebody. I could not afford to give up a day's work to come around and tell you about it, but I knew I must tell somebody and I did not know anybody I would so like to tell as you. I know you won't be angry." Indeed, I was not angry. I was glad she had come, and rejoiced with her, that old washerwoman filled with the Holy Spirit and so full of joy that, poor as she was, she had to give up a day's work to go and tell somebody she loved all about it.

Before I came to believe on the Lord Jesus Christ I was one of the bluest men who ever lived. I would sit down by the hour and brood. I have never known what the blues mean since the day I really became a Christian, absolutely surrendered to God. I have had troubles. I have had losses. There have been times in my life when I have lost pretty much everything the world holds dear. I know what it is to have a wife and four children, and to lose everything of a financial kind I had in the world, and not know from meal to meal where the next meal was coming from. I was absolutely without resources, living from hand to mouth □ from God's hand to my mouth. I have known what it is to be with a wife and child in a foreign country where they spoke a strange language, and for some reason or other supplies did not come, and I did not know anyone in the city well enough to turn to for help; but I did not worry. I knew it was all in God's hands, that it would all come out right somehow, and of course it did come out right.

The first time I ever visited London, thirty-nine years ago last September, I was planning to spend two weeks in England, and then start for America. I expected to find money waiting for me I when I reached London, and I reached London with a wife and child, and not a letter and no money. But I said, "The letter and the money will come tomorrow or the next day." My wife made some purchases, taking it for granted we would have money when the purchases came home; but the money did not come. Day after day passed, and the dresses came home and it was about time for the landlady to come with her board bill. It came to be the very last day before our boat started, and not a penny in sight. I went down to the bank. I did not know a soul in London. There were three or four million people there then a stranger amid three or four million people, money absolutely gone, three thousand miles from friends. I did not worry. I knew the money would come. I did not know how it would come, for the source I expected to receive it from seemed utterly cut off; but yet I was happy. Why? Because I was a child of God; I had the promises of the Bible; I knew they were absolutely certain. I never lost an hour's sleep. I never worried. I just trusted. It seemed as though I would have to be fed somewhat as Elijah was, but I knew I would be fed. I knew my wife and child would be provided for. The money came, and I sailed on the steamer I expected to sail on, with every penny due paid, and money in my pocket. Friends, a Christian is happy at all times and under all circumstances. We rejoice with "inexpressible and glorious joy" every one of the twenty-four hours of the day that we are awake, and sometimes in our sleep. You, too, can have that joy.

How to Get This Inexpressible and Glorious Joy

Now arises the question, "What must anyone here tonight who does not have this inexpressible and glorious joy do to get it?" I have really answered that question several times in what I have already said, but to be sure that we all really understand it, let me answer it again, or rather let my text answer it, "Though you have not seen him, you love him; and even though you do not see him now, you believe in him and are filled with an inexpressible and glorious joy." The text tells us that the way to obtain this "inexpressible and glorious joy," the way to be inexpressibly happy at all times and under all circumstances, is just by believing on the unseen Christ Jesus. What does it mean to believe on Jesus Christ? There is no mystery at all about that. It simply means to put confidence in Jesus Christ to be what He claims to be and what He offers Himself to be to us, to put confidence in Him as the One who died in our place, the One who bore our sins in His own body on the cross, and to trust God to forgive us all our sins because Jesus Christ died in our place; to put confidence in Him as the One who was raised from the dead and who now has "all power in heaven and on earth," and therefore is able to keep us day by day, and give us victory over sin, and to trust this risen Christ to give us victory over sin day by day; and to put confidence in Him as our absolute Lord and Master, and therefore to surrender our thoughts and wills and lives entirely to His control, believing everything He says, even though every scholar on earth denies it, obeying everything He commands, whatever it may cost; and to put confidence in Him as our Divine Lord, and confess Him as Lord before the world, and worship and adore Him. It is wonderful the joy that comes to him who thus believes on Jesus Christ. But one must really believe on Jesus Christ to have this joy.

Merely being a member of a church is not enough. Merely being baptized is not enough. Merely reading your Bible is not enough. Merely praying is not enough. Merely going to church is not enough. Merely going to the Lord's table and partaking of the Lord's Supper is not enough. But if you are a real believer on Jesus Christ, if you have put all your trust in the Lord Jesus as your atoning Savior and your risen Savior, and your risen Lord and Master, and surrendered your thoughts and life to Him utterly as your Lord and Master, and are confessing Him as such before the world, if you have thrown your heart's door wide open for the Lord Jesus to come in, and live, and rule, and reign there, you will have "inexpressible and glorious joy" at all times and under all circumstances.

All anyone has to do, then, to be inexpressibly happy at all times and under all circumstances, is to believe on Jesus Christ. It does not make any difference what his circumstances may be: he may be rich or he may be poor; he may be highly educated, or he may be ignorant; he may be in good health or he may be a hopeless invalid; he may have been a moral, clean, upright man, or he may have been the vilest of sinners, it matters not. Everyone who believes on the unseen but living Christ will find "inexpressible and glorious joy." I can bring scores, hundreds, thousands of witnesses to prove that. You cannot bring a single witness on the other side. Col. Robert Ingersoll delighted to say, "It doesn't make one happy to be a Christian." How did he know? He never tried it. You can search the earth through and you cannot find me one single man or woman who was ever an out-and-out believer in Jesus Christ, a real wholehearted believer in Jesus Christ, one who had surrendered all to Jesus Christ; I say you cannot find me even one such man or woman who will deny that Jesus Christ gives "inexpressible and glorious joy" to those who thus believe on Him. Here, then, is the way the case stands: Every single competent witness, that is, every witness who has ever tried it, testifies that believing in Jesus Christ does bring "inexpressible and glorious joy," and these witnesses number thousands, tens of thousands and hundreds of thousands, people from every rank of society and culture, and not one witness on the other side. Is it demonstrated or not? It certainly is.

I take it that I am speaking tonight to reasonable men and women. You desire "inexpressible and glorious joy." I have told you how to get it. There can be no doubt about it. The evidence is overwhelmingly convincing. There is, then, but one rational thing for you to do, believe on Jesus Christ tonight. Will you do it?

Once a man who was utterly miserable came to me. He was a rarely gifted man, a brilliant scholar, but utterly miserable. If ever I saw a man in hell he was the man. He had attempted suicide at least four times. He had been so near succeeding in his attempts that on two occasions it had been necessary to pump out of him the poison he had taken and thus bring him back to life. I urged him to believe on Jesus Christ. He replied, "I cannot, I have sinned away the Day of Grace." Day after day I talked with the man and always I had but one message, and that was, "Come to Jesus Christ. Believe on Jesus Christ." At last, one day the man did come to Jesus Christ. He found "inexpressible and glorious joy." Sometimes I have seen that man when his face was radiant. Out of hell into heaven by just believing on Jesus Christ! Will you take that same step now?

※

Also Available from This Publisher